Gifts Galore!

Recipes to Make & Give In-A-Jar

Sweets, Soups,
Snacks & More
for All Occasions

In these pages, you'll find all kinds of gift ideas to inspire your creativity! Whatever the gift-giving occasion, you can find the perfect one-of-a-kind recipe here. Hostess gifts, an addition for a wedding shower, a gift of appreciation for someone who does a favor, and over 60 ideas for year-round holidays.

From soups and salads to sweets and snacks, *Gifts Galore* is your go-to resource for giving wonderful tasting treats in a wonderfully tasteful way!

Table of Contents

Table of Contents

SWEET CINNAMON POPCORN

Ingredients:

1 Tbsp granulated sugar
1 tsp fine or table salt
1/2 tsp ground cinnamon
2 Tbsp coconut oil
1/3 cup popcorn kernels
1/2 to 1 vanilla bean, split and seeds scraped away

Directions:

Mix the sugar, salt, and cinnamon together in a small bowl and set aside. Heat the coconut oil in a large heavy pot or a stovetop popcorn popper for 1 minute. Add 2 popcorn kernels. Once they pop, add the scraped vanilla seeds and stir. Immediately dump in the remaining popcorn kernels, then quickly stir in the sugar-cinnamon mixture. Cover the pot, leaving the lid slightly askew (and facing away from you) to allow steam to escape. Shake the pot back and forth over the burner so the popcorn doesn't burn. Keep shaking until most of the popcorn has popped and you hear 1 - 2 seconds between pops. Immediately turn off the heat, uncover the pot, and carefully dump the popcorn out onto a baking sheet or into a paper bag. Let cool and then put into airtight jars or containers for gift giving.

Attach a cinnamon stick to your gift jar for a sweet-spicy-smelling fall or winter gift.

TOFFEE NUT POPCORN

Ingredients:

5 cups of popped popcorn or 1 large bag regular popped popcorn
1/2 cup toasted pecan halves and pieces
1/2 cup whole, toasted almonds
1/2 cup whole cashews
2/3 cup brown sugar, firmly packed
1/2 cup butter
1/4 cup light corn syrup
1/4 tsp cream of tartar
1/4 tsp baking soda
1/4 tsp almond extract
1/4 tsp butter flavoring

Directions:

Spray an 11"x13" pan with non-stick cooking spray. In a large bowl, combine the nuts and the popped popcorn. In a saucepan, combine the brown sugar, butter, corn syrup and cream of tartar. Stir constantly until sugar has melted and a candy thermometer reaches 300-310°. Remove from the heat. Stir in baking soda and extract and flavoring. Pour this candy mixture over the popcorn and stir gently. Dump candied popcorn mixture into the prepared pan and let cool before breaking into smaller chunks.

Spoon the popcorn into glass jars tied with ribbon and decorated with sprigs of holly (at Christmas) or a couple of freshly cut flowers.

A LITTLE BIT OF SUGAR (ALMOND CRUNCH)

Ingredients:

1 cup whole almonds
2 cups pretzels
1 cup dried, sweetened cranberries
1 egg white, whipped until foamy
1/2 cup cinnamon sugar mix
(1/2 cup sugar, 1/2 tsp cinnamon, 1/2 tsp salt)

Directions:

Preheat oven to 350°. Spray a cookie sheet with non-stick cooking spray. Roast almonds on cookie sheet for 7-8 minutes then turn oven down to 225°. In a large bowl, mix the almonds, pretzels, and cranberries. Pour the whipped egg white over the mixture. Use hands to mix until completely coated. Sprinkle the cinnamon sugar mix over the almond mixture and stir. Spread onto the cookie sheet and bake for 60 minutes, stirring every 15 minutes. Let cool then store in an airtight container.

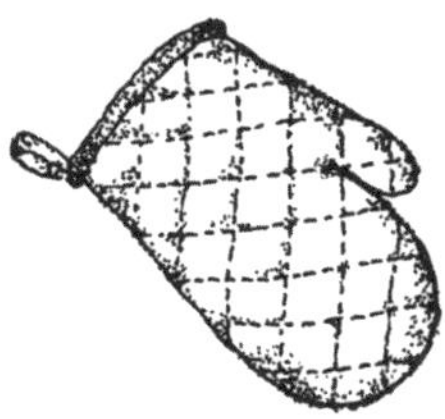

WHITE CHOCOLATE PIZZA (BY THE SLICE)

Ingredients:
12 oz quality white chocolate, finely chopped
1/4 cup dried cranberries, blueberries, cherries and/or apricots
1/4 cup toasted pecans
1/4 cup sliced almonds
1/4 cup dried crystallized ginger, diced

Directions:
Spray an 8"x 8" baking pan with non-stick cooking spray. Place the white chocolate in a microwave-safe bowl and microwave on high, stopping to stir every 15-30 seconds until it has melted. When it has reached a smooth consistency, spread it into the prepared pan. Evenly sprinkle the fruits and nuts over the top, and then press gently into the chocolate. Refrigerate until firm, about 30 minutes. Break the chocolate into triangle shaped pieces (pizza slices) and store in an airtight container.

Just like your favorite pizza, this candy can be topped with your choice of yummy treats. Be creative! Give it in a jar tied with ribbons, or in a basket with some seasonal fresh fruit.

SUGARED DATE-NUT BALLS

Ingredients:
3/4 cup butter
3/4 cup sugar
1 lb dates
1 cup pecans, chopped
1 cup crispy rice cereal
Additional sugar

Directions:
In a medium saucepan, melt butter, add the sugar and dates. Bring to a boil and cook for 3 minutes, stirring constantly. Add the pecans and cereal, stirring to coat. Cool enough to be able to roll into small balls. Pour some sugar into a bowl and roll each date ball around in the sugar until completely covered. Place on waxed paper to finish cooling. Store in an airtight container.

Fill a 1 quart jar with date balls, or use a pretty gift box, lined with waxed paper. Tie the top with a ribbon and attach the recipe and a note saying "Happy Retirement!" (or Birthday, Anniversary, eg...).

CRUNCHY PUMPKIN PIE SNACK MIX

Ingredients:
1/4 cup brown sugar
1 Tbsp pumpkin pie spice
1/4 cup butter
2 tsp vanilla
2 cups crunchy cinnamon flavored rice squares cereal
2 cups crunchy wheat squares cereal
2 cups crunchy honey nut flavored squares cereal
8 oz chopped pecans
1 cup sweetened, dried cranberries
1 cup tri-colored candy corn candy

Directions:
In a small bowl, combine the brown sugar and pumpkin pie spice; set aside. In another small dish, microwave butter until melted. Stir in vanilla. In a large bowl, mix all cereals and pecans. Pour butter mixture over cereal mixture, stirring until evenly distributed. Add sugar and spice mixture and stir until coated. Microwave the cereal mixture uncovered, for 5 minutes or until mixture begins to brown, stirring every minute. Spread on wax paper or a cookie sheet to cool. Add the cranberries and candy, and store in an airtight container.

Glue a 3" wide strip of burlap around the middle of a jar. Tie a piece of jute or an autumn colored ribbon around the middle of the burlap and attach a printed label to it.

SWEET AND SMOKY NUT CUPS

Ingredients:
1 cup brown sugar
1/4 cup fresh rosemary leaves
1 Tbsp butter, melted
2 tsp ground cumin
1/2 tsp cayenne pepper
1 large egg white
1 Tbsp water
6 oz pecan halves (about 1 1/2 cups)
6 oz raw almonds
4 oz smoked almonds (about 1 cup)
Salt and pepper to taste

Directions:
Preheat oven to 275°. In a large bowl, whisk together the brown sugar, rosemary, butter, cumin, cayenne, and paprika. Whisk egg white and water in a medium bowl until foamy. Add nuts to egg white mixture and toss to coat. Drain any excess egg mixture and add nuts to the spice mixture and toss again to coat. Spread in an even layer on a baking sheet covered with parchment paper. Bake in oven, stirring every 15 minutes for 45 minutes. Let cool and store in an airtight container.

TRAIL MIX FOR THE WHOLE CREW

Ingredients:

Layer the following ingredients in a large glass jar:

- 1 cup of honey nut oat cereal
- 1 cup of small pretzels
- 1 cup of cheese flavored crackers (fish-shaped)
- 1 cup of peanut butter cookie bites
- 1 cup of oatmeal cereal squares
- 1 cup of animal shaped crackers
- 1 cup of dried, sweetened cranberries
- 1/2 cup of each: dried apricots, bananas, and apples

Include a note with directions for recipient:

Pour the jar ingredients into a large bowl and stir to combine. Separate into baggies for your next outdoor adventure!

This is a favorite gift for outdoorsy families with young children. Adults love it because it provides both carbohydrates and protein to keep everyone energized; children love it because it really tastes good.

CHEESE CRACKERS

Ingredients:
8 oz sharp cheddar cheese, coarsely shredded
1/4 cup (1/2 stick butter), room temperature
1/2 tsp salt
1 cup pastry flour
2 Tbsp ice water, more as needed

Directions:
Preheat the oven to 375°. Cream the cheese, butter, and salt until combined. Add the flour, then slowly add the water until the dough forms a ball. Pat the dough in a disk and put in the fridge for an hour. Roll out the dough until it's 1/8" thick and, using a pastry cutter, cut 1" squares. Put on a cookie sheet and poke holes in each square with a fork or end of a straw. Bake for 12 minutes.

These crackers go with everything!
Place a jar of the crackers in a basket with
some shrimp and crab dip, or a cucumber (to slice),
some creamy goat cheese,
and a small jar of toasted pecans.

CAJUN TRAIL MIX

Ingredients:
1/2 cup whole raw almonds
1/2 cup pecan halves
1/2 cup walnut halves
1/4 cup shelled sunflower seeds
1/4 cup shelled pumpkin seeds
2 Tbsp canola oil
1/4 tsp garlic powder
1/4 tsp chili powder
1/4 tsp ground cumin
2 pinches cayenne pepper

Directions:
Preheat oven to 350°. In a large bowl, combine all the ingredients and toss well to coat. Spread the nuts in a single layer on a baking sheet and bake, shaking them every few minutes, until toasted and fragrant, about 15 minutes. Let the nuts cool and store in an airtight container.

ORANGE CHIPOTLE-SPICED PECAN MIX

Ingredients:
1 Tbsp grated orange rind
1 Tbsp fresh orange juice
1 large egg white
2 cups pecan halves
1 Tbsp brown sugar
1 tsp sea salt
1/2 tsp ground chipotle chile pepper
1/2 cup dried, sweetened cranberries

Directions:
Preheat oven to 225°. Spray a cookie sheet or jelly roll pan with non-stick cooking spray. In a medium bowl, whisk together the orange peel, orange juice, and egg white. Stir in the pecans. Combine the sugar, salt, and pepper. Add to pecan mixture, stirring to blend. Spread the nut mixture evenly on the prepared pan. Bake for 1 hour, stirring occasionally. Remove from oven. When cooled, stir in the cranberries. Store in an airtight container for up to one week.

Pour your mixture into a glass jar and tie it with a length of fabric lace. Write a special message on a "chalkboard" label and add to the jar for a rustic look.

MOUTHWATERING MINESTRONE

Ingredients:

4 cups beef stock
1 1/2 cups water
2 14.5-oz cans diced tomatoes
1 cup celery, diced
1 cup carrots, diced
1 cup yellow onion, diced
4 cloves garlic, minced
1 15-oz can dark red kidney beans, drained and rinsed
1 15-oz can white navy beans or cannellini beans, drained and rinsed
1 15-oz can Italian green beans, drained
1 Tbsp fresh parsley, chopped
2 tsp dried basil or 1 Tbsp fresh basil
1/2 tsp dried thyme
1/2 tsp dried crushed rosemary
2 bay leaves
1/2 tsp sugar
Salt and freshly ground black pepper, to taste
1 1/3 cups zucchini, diced
1 1/3 cups shell, elbow or rotini pasta
2 cups slightly packed fresh spinach, chopped
1 cup cream

Directions:

Combine all except zucchini, pasta, fresh spinach and cream in a crock pot and cook on low for 6-8 hours. Add the final 4 ingredients and cook an additional 15 minutes. Spoon into glass jars and refrigerate or freeze.

A jar of delicious soup with a warm, fresh loaf of artisan bread makes a healthy, hearty gift.

INDIAN LENTIL SOUP

Ingredients:
1/2 pound red lentils
Seasoned salt
3 Tbsp minced dried onion
1 Tbsp curry powder
1 tsp ground cumin
1 tsp garlic powder
1 Tbsp fresh ginger, chopped fine
1/2 pound green lentils
5 oz dried apples, cut into 1/2" pieces
1 Tbsp dried parsley leaves
Pinch of cayenne pepper, cinnamon, ground cloves

Directions:
Layer above ingredients in a jar, in the order given. Seal lid tightly. Attach a label to the jar of ingredients with the following instructions:

Indian Lentil Soup
Place lentil soup mix in 3 quart saucepan with 7 cups water. Heat to boiling on high. Reduce heat to low; cover and simmer 20 - 30 minutes, stirring occasionally. Makes 8 cups soup.

FEEL-BETTER-SOON CHICKEN SOUP

Ingredients:

1 large onion, chopped
1 cup celery, chopped
1 cup carrots, sliced
1 cup peas
1 cup chicken breast, cooked and cut into bite size pieces
4 tsp chicken bullion granules
1 fresh sprig of thyme
2 bay leaves
2 fresh sprigs of parsley
Seal the lid of jar tightly. Refrigerate or freeze immediately, keep chilled until ready to use.

TO MAKE JAR GIFT:

Layer the following ingredients in a 1 quart jar:

Attach this recipe to your gift:

Put jar ingredients into a crock pot along with 6 cups of water. Heat on low for 6 hours or until carrots are tender. During the last hour add a package of home-style noodles (in the grocery freezer case).

For a get-well gift, put the jar of soup ingredients, with directions, in a basket. Include a pack of teas and honey, a crossword book, a magazine or inspirational reading.

LOGGING CAMP POTATO SOUP

Ingredients:
1 stick of butter
1/2 cup celery, chopped fine
1 cup onion, chopped fine
3 medium potatoes, chopped
1/4 cup flour
1 cup milk
2 1/2 cups chicken broth
Salt and pepper to taste
1 cup cream
Cheddar cheese

Directions:
Melt butter in a saucepan, add celery, onions, and potatoes. Sauté 10 minutes then add the flour. Cook, stirring for 30 seconds. Gradually add the milk and chicken broth, stirring until boiling. Simmer for 30 minutes, remove from heat and cool slightly. Purée in batches in a blender or food processor. Return to saucepan. Over medium heat add salt, pepper, cream and cheese. Stir until cheese melts. Eat immediately or pour into an airtight container and refrigerate.

Put a jar of potato soup ingredients into a fabric lined basket. Include in the basket small containers of shredded cheese, bacon pieces (cooked), and chopped green onion. A loaf of Sheepherder's bread and the soup recipe will round out the gift basket.

PERFECT ITALIAN SALAD

Ingredients:
Balsamic Vinegar
Olive oil
Fresh tomatoes, sliced
Black olives
Prosciutto slices
Fresh mozzarella cheese, sliced
Fresh basil leaves

Directions:
Layer above ingredients in a jar, adding as much or as little of each as you prefer. You can make individual salads in 1 pint jars, or a larger salad for a group in a 1 quart jar. Store in the refrigerator. Turn the jar upside down before serving to disperse the dressing.

For a layered salad jar, attach a baggie of homemade croutons or toasted almonds to the lid with a ribbon.

PICNIC BEAN SALAD

Ingredients:

3/4 cup olive oil
1/4 cup balsamic vinegar
1/4 cup red wine vinegar
1/2 tsp seasoned salt
1/2 tsp ground black pepper
1/2 cup white sugar
1 15-oz can green beans, drained
1 15-oz can wax beans, drained
1 15-oz can garbanzo beans, rinsed and drained
1 15-oz can kidney beans, rinsed and drained
1 15-oz can black beans, rinsed and drained
1 15-oz can white corn
1/2 cup onion, chopped
1/2 cup celery, chopped

Directions:

In a large bowl, combine the oil, vinegars, salt, pepper, and sugar. Whisk together until sugar has dissolved. Add the rest of the ingredients to the bowl and stir to combine, making sure everything is covered with the dressing. Spoon into jars and store in the refrigerator. Marinate overnight before indulging!

Take two jars of this delicious salad as a thoughtful hostess gift to a summer barbeque or picnic. By giving two jars, the hostess can open one to be used immediately and save one for later. Tie a red and white checked ribbon around the lid in keeping with the picnic theme.

LAYERED SUMMER SALAD

Ingredients:
1 cup iceberg lettuce, chopped
1 cup baby spinach leaves, chopped
2-3 hardboiled eggs, peeled and sliced
6 strips bacon, cooked crispy and cut into pieces
1-2 tomatoes, diced
Green onion, chopped
Cheddar cheese, shredded
Peas, partially thawed
1/4 cup mayonnaise
1/4 cup sour cream
2 tsp sugar

Directions:
Layer all ingredients in a 1 quart jar except for the last 3. In a small bowl, combine the mayonnaise, sour cream, and sugar. Spread the dressing over the top of the peas and all the way to the edge of the container. Cover and refrigerate. Just before serving, toss to combine ingredients.

For salad gift jars, tie a pair of salad tongs to the lid of the jar along with the recipe for the salad.

FRESH CARROT SALAD

Ingredients:
4 cups fresh carrots, shredded
1 cup raisins
1 cup fresh pineapple, cut into bite size pieces
1/2 cup mayonnaise
1/4 cup plain Greek yogurt
1 Tbsp sugar
2 tsp lemon juice

Directions:
In a large bowl, stir together the carrots, raisins and pineapple. Combine the final 4 ingredients and add to bowl. Refrigerate in an airtight container.

Makes a nice hostess gift for a springtime luncheon or Easter potluck.

MEXICAN PASTA SALAD

Ingredients:

1 cup black beans, drained and rinsed
1 can white corn, drained
1/2 cup sweet red onion, chopped
1/2 cup black olives, sliced
1 cup sweet green or red pepper, diced
1 cup cherry tomatoes, halved
3 cups bowtie pasta, cooked
1/2 cup mayonnaise
1/2 cup sour cream
1 package of taco seasoning

Directions:

In a 1 quart glass jar, layer the first 7 ingredients. Seal lid tightly and refrigerate. In a bowl, mix together the mayonnaise, sour cream, and seasoning. Pour the dressing into a small container and refrigerate until ready to serve. To make the salad, pour the jar ingredients into a large bowl and drizzle dressing over the top. Stir to coat.

This salad looks so pretty layered in the jar, it is a delight to give! Place the jar into a Mexican patterned salad bowl (padded with shredded paper filler) alongside a cruet filled with the dressing and salad tongs. Don't forget to write out the recipe and include it as well.

GARDEN FRESH BASIL PESTO

Perfect on pasta or chicken, this makes a delicious veggie pizza or pasta sauce.

Ingredients:
2 cloves garlic
1/2 tsp salt
1 tsp black pepper
1 cup roasted pine nuts
2/3 to 1 cup olive oil
2 cups packed fresh basil, washed
1 cup Parmesan cheese

Directions:
In a food processor, grind 2 cloves of garlic, the salt, pepper, the pine nuts, and 1/3 cup of the olive oil. Add the basil and process to a thin paste. Add the parmesan cheese. Drizzle in more olive oil and process to a thick paste.

A jar of this pesto makes a lovely hostess gift. Or you can create a complete kitchen gift by placing the jar in a pretty colander lined with a cloth, along with a package of homemade-style pasta and a fresh baguette.

SWEET AND SPICY SUMMER SALSA

Ingredients:

3 large peaches
1 can of white shoe peg corn
1 yellow bell pepper
1 orange bell pepper
1 red bell pepper
1/2 pound roasted green chilies
2 jalapeno peppers
2 garlic cloves
2 Tbsp white vinegar
2 Tbsp fresh cilantro, chopped
1 Tbsp Worcestershire sauce
3 large tomatoes
1 Tbsp lime juice
1-2 Tbsp olive oil
Salt and pepper to taste

Directions:

Peel and chop the peaches into 1/4" pieces and put into a mixing bowl. Drain the can of corn and add it to the peaches. Set aside. Chop the bell peppers and green chillies very fine and add to the corn. Slice jalapenos in half, remove seeds and vein. Mince in food processor with the garlic clove and vinegar. Drain the vinegar from the food processer bowl and add the jalapeno and garlic mixture to the vegetable mixture. Add the cilantro, the Worcestershire sauce, lime juice and oil. Season with salt and pepper.

This is such a pretty salsa, it looks beautiful in a glass jar. To add a special touch, try making your own homemade tamales or tortilla chips from flour tortillas. Wrap them in foil and put in a basket with the jar of salsa.

SOUTH-OF-THE-BORDER GRILLING MARINADE

Ingredients:

1/2 onion
1 large garlic clove
1/4 cup olive oil
1/2 tsp fresh oregano, chopped
1/2 tsp cumin
1 tsp salt
1/2 tsp black pepper
1/4 tsp dried chipotle powder
1/2 tsp red pepper flakes
2 Tbsp lime juice
1 handful cilantro leaves, chopped

Directions:

Put all marinade ingredients in the blender or food processor and liquefy. Store marinade in an airtight container in the refrigerator for up to one week. When ready to use, put meat pieces into a large plastic bag. Pour enough marinade into bag to cover the meat, seal the bag. Refrigerate for at least 4 hours, discard marinade, and grill. Especially delicious with chicken.

Pour marinade into a 1 quart jar, seal the lid tightly, and put in a basket with a jar of Homemade BBQ Sauce (recipe on next page), grilling utensils and barbeque themed napkins.

BBQ SAUCE

Ingredients:

1 onion, chopped
1 clove garlic, chopped
1/2 cup golden raisins, chopped
1/4 cup cocktail sauce
1 cup ketchup
2 Tbsp cider vinegar
1 Tbsp molasses
2/3 cup butter, softened
1/2 tsp basil
1 Tbsp chili powder
1/2 tsp rosemary
1/2 tsp thyme
1/2 tsp marjoram
1 tsp salt
1/4 cup brown sugar
1 Tbsp lemon juice

Directions:

Place the onion, garlic, raisins, cocktail sauce, and ketchup in a blender or food processor and process until thoroughly blended, then transfer to a saucepan. Put all additional ingredients in the saucepan and bring to a boil, stirring constantly. Simmer for 1 hour or more, stirring occasionally. Pour into a jar and refrigerate. This sauce gets even better after the flavors have had a chance to mingle for a couple of days. Store in the fridge or can be frozen.

Pour this special Barbeque Sauce into a glass jar and seal lid tightly. Tie a ribbon around the jar and place in a basket with a package of plastic BBQ bibs (available at kitchen specialty stores) and a red-and-white check hot pad or grilling apron.

MEXICAN CHIP DIP

Ingredients:

1/2 cup dried parsley
1/3 cup minced onion
1/4 cup dried chives
1/3 cup chili powder
1/4 cup ground cumin
1/4 cup salt

In a large bowl, combine the spices and store in an airtight glass jar or container.

Attach this recipe to your gift:

Easy Mexican Chip Dip
In a medium mixing bowl whisk together 3 Tbsp of this Dip Mix with 1 cup mayonnaise and 1 cup plain Greek yogurt. Whisk the mixture until smooth. Refrigerate for 2 - 4 hours. Serve with tortilla chips or fresh vegetables.

Put a jar of this seasoning mix in a basket with a bag of Tortilla Chips. You might consider also including a jar of Sweet and Spicy Summer Salsa for added variety. Tie a ribbon around the whole basket and be sure to include the recipes.

HOT FUDGE SUNDAE SAUCE

Ingredients:

1 3/4 cups heavy cream
1/2 cup granulated sugar
1/4 cup brown sugar
1/4 cup butter, cut into small pieces
2 3/4 cups semisweet chocolate chips
1/8 tsp salt
1 tsp vanilla extract

Directions:

In a heavy saucepan over low heat, bring the cream just to a boil, then add the sugars and stir until dissolved. Add the butter, stirring until completely melted, then stir in the chocolate chips. When chocolate has become soft, stir it in gently. Remove from heat and stir in the salt and vanilla extract. Cool and store in the refrigerator in a glass jar.

Give in a basket with a set of ice cream bowls or tall sundae glasses. Include a small jar of nuts, and some fresh strawberries or bananas.

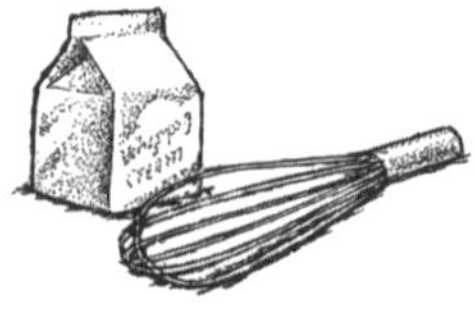

SOUTHERN CARAMEL CREAM

Ingredients:
1 1/4 cups sugar
1/4 cup brown sugar
1/2 cup water
1 cup whipping cream
1/2 cup butter, cut into pieces
1/2 tsp vanilla extract

Directions:
Combine sugars and water in a heavy saucepan, cooking and stirring until sugars dissolve. Increase heat to medium-high, and boil gently, without stirring, until syrup turns a deep amber color, about 8 minutes. Gradually add the cream (sauce will bubble up vigorously). Add the butter, stirring until smooth. Remove from heat, and stir in vanilla. Pour into an airtight container and cool.

Of course this caramel sauce is delicious on ice cream, but it's amazing drizzled on a piece of warm apple cake topped with whipped cream, or a bowl of piping hot oatmeal, it adds a little something extra to a slice of cheesecake, or as a topping on banana-filled crepes. Give it in a pretty glass jar with a recipe label and some of these yummy suggestions.

ORANGE CARAMEL SAUCE WITH PECAN PRALINE

Ingredients:

2 cups sugar
1/3 cup water
1/4 cup frozen orange juice concentrate, thawed
1/2 cup whole pecans, toasted (about 2 1/2 oz)
2/3 cup heavy cream
2 Tbsp butter
2 tsp orange zest

Directions:

Spray a cookie sheet with non-stick cooking spray. Combine the first 3 ingredients in a medium saucepan and stir over medium heat until sugar dissolves. Cook until mixture turns a deep amber caramel, about 15 minutes. Remove from heat and pour half of this caramel into a smaller saucepan. Working quickly with the smaller pan, prepare the Pecan Praline by adding pecans and stirring until coated. Pour the mixture onto the prepared cookie sheet, spreading evenly. Allow to cool completely. Meanwhile, add cream and butter to remaining hot caramel in the medium saucepan. Boil until smooth and slightly thickened, stirring occasionally, for about 5 minutes. Stir in orange zest. Transfer sauce to jar and cool.

A perfect gift for ice cream lovers!
Prepare two separate jars, one with caramel sauce and the other with pecan praline, then wrap in colorful cellophane and ribbons.

APPLE CHEESE SPREAD

Ingredients:
8 oz cream cheese, softened
1/2 cup mayonnaise
1/2 sharp cheddar cheese, grated
1/2 cup Granny Smith apples, chopped
2 Tbsp honey
1/4 tsp cinnamon

Directions:
Combine cream cheese and mayonnaise until well blended. Add the grated cheese, apples, honey and cinnamon. Mix well and chill in refrigerator.

Spoon the Apple Cheese Spread into a 1 pint jar and seal tightly. Label with the recipe and tie a ribbon around the lid. Make it extra special by including it in a basket with a box of gourmet crackers and a decorative cheese spreader. Note: When gifting this recipe, make very sure it stays cold and is returned to a refrigerator quickly.

SHRIMP AND CRAB DIP

Ingredients:

2 3-oz packages of cream cheese, softened
1 can cream of mushroom soup
1/4 cup green onion, minced fine
1 cup mayonnaise
1 cup celery, chopped fine
1 cup small cocktail shrimp, fully cooked, tails removed
1 cup crabmeat, drained, flaked, and cartilage removed, or imitation crab, chopped

Directions:

In large bowl, stir together the cream cheese, soup, and onion. Melt in the microwave in 15 second intervals, stirring until well blended. Add the mayonnaise, celery, shrimp and crab, stirring to combine. Spoon into an airtight container and refrigerate.

This dip is delicious and elegant served with a variety of crackers or vegetables. Spoon dip into an airtight glass jar and give it along with a box of variety crackers and a decorative little knife for spreading.

BLUE CHEESE BASIL DIP

Ingredients:

8 oz cream cheese, softened
1/2 cup sour cream
Salt and pepper to taste
1/2 cup fresh basil, chopped fine
1/2 cup pecans, toasted and chopped
1 cup blue cheese, crumbled
1/2 cup chives, minced

Directions:

In a small bowl, combine the cream cheese and sour cream. Add salt and pepper, basil, and pecans, stirring to combine. Gently stir in the blue cheese and chives. Spoon into an airtight container and refrigerate. This dip goes well with sweet fruits such as apples, pears, or peach slices, or vegetables such as celery sticks, carrots, cucumber slices or zucchini.

Place the jar of dip in a basket filled with some apples and pears. Tie a pretty serving spoon to the lid of the jar with a ribbon.

CINNAMON HONEY BUTTER

Ingredients:
2 cups honey
2 cups butter, softened
2 cups powdered sugar
4 tsp cinnamon
1/2 tsp nutmeg
1/8 tsp allspice

Directions:
Using an electric mixer, blend all ingredients until smooth and creamy. Pour into an airtight container and refrigerate.

Wrap the jar of Cinnamon Honey Butter in tissue paper or gift wrap. Place it in a basket with a honey crock, a wooden honey dipper, and a loaf of fresh bread.

YUMMY HUMMUS

Ingredients:

2 15-oz cans of garbanzo beans, rinsed
2 large cloves of garlic, peeled
1/4 cup lemon juice
2 heaping Tbsp tahini (sesame paste)
1/2 tsp salt (make sure to taste at the end and add more if necessary)
1/3 cup olive oil
1/3 cup water

Directions:

Combine the beans, garlic, lemon juice, tahini and salt in the bowl of a food processor or in a blender. Pulse 5 - 6 times before blending completely. With the food processor running, pour in the olive oil. If needed, add water, a little at a time until it is the desired consistency. Remove from the food processor, salt to taste, and store in an airtight container in the refrigerator.

Place half of the finished hummus in a small jar, set aside. Add additional seasonings to the second half and then blend. Options include tuna and olives, sun dried tomatoes and basil, or try a dash of cayenne pepper to spice it up a bit. This way you can give 2 small jars of different flavored hummus. It makes a lovely gift when tucked in a gift bag with a box of specialty crackers or pita chips.

MEDITERRANEAN SALSA

Ingredients:

1 6.5-oz jar marinated artichoke hearts, chopped, reserve liquid
1 garlic clove, pressed
2 Tbsp capers
1/2 cup canned white beans, drained and rinsed
1/2 cup pitted black olives, chopped
1/4 cup red onion, chopped
3 medium plum or Roma tomatoes, chopped
2 Tbsp fresh basil, finely chopped
1 Tbsp olive oil
Salt and pepper to taste

Directions:

Reserve 2-3 Tbsp liquid from artichoke hearts, drain rest of the liquid. In a large bowl, combine all ingredients except the olive oil, salt and pepper. Stir together. Drizzle olive oil over the top and season to taste. Refrigerate for 2 hours or longer before serving.

This dip is especially good with pita chips. Make homemade pita chips by toasting slices of buttered pita bread in the oven until crispy. Salt lightly, if desired. Put the chips into a cellophane bag and include them with the jar of dip.

SWEET & TART HOLIDAY DIP

Ingredients:
1 cup water
1 cup sugar
1 12-oz package fresh cranberries
1/2 cup raspberry pomegranate preserves
1 8-oz package cream cheese

Directions:
Combine water and sugar in a saucepan and bring to a boil. Boil for about 5 minutes. Add the cranberries and cook until the berries pop, stirring until the sauce thickens. Remove from heat and stir in the preserves. Cool and then refrigerate in an air tight container. Serve over the cream cheese, with crackers on the side.

Spoon into a glass jar and seal the lid tightly. String some "jingle bells" onto a thin ribbon, attach the recipe and tie the ribbon around the lid.

SMOKY SALMON SPREAD

Ingredients:

1 8-oz package cream cheese, softened
1/4 cup plain Greek yogurt
1 tsp Worcestershire sauce
6 oz smoked salmon, chopped
1/2 cup pecans, chopped
2 green onions, diced
1 Tbsp dill, chopped
1 tsp lemon juice
dash of hot sauce

Directions:

Using an electric mixer, combine all ingredients and blend until well mixed. Spoon into an airtight container and refrigerate. Serve with bagel chips, carrot and celery sticks, or fresh artisan bread.

Put this spread in an attractive small size crock or glass jar with a tightly fitting lid and a decorative spreader. Add a loaf of bread or bag of bagel chips. Save yourself some time and include the recipe, too—this spread is so addicting, it won't last long and your friends will be wanting more!

FLUFFY FRUIT DIP

Ingredients:

1 8-oz package cream cheese, softened
1 7-oz container of marshmallow creme
1/2 tsp vanilla extract

Directions:

Using an electric mixer, combine the ingredients until smooth. Serve with fruit.

Fill a basket with an assortment of fresh fruit—strawberries, bananas, pears, grapes, apples or your favorite fruit. Spoon the dip into a glass jar and seal the lid tightly. Place the jar in the middle of the fruit basket.

CANDY CANE BITES

Ingredients:

17 oz white chocolate, finely chopped
30 red-and-white-striped hard peppermint candies, coarsely crushed
7 oz semisweet chocolate chips
6 Tbsp whipping cream
1/2 tsp peppermint extract

Directions:

Cover the inside of a 9"x 13" baking pan with foil. Put the white chocolate in the top of a double boiler (or use a metal bowl set over a saucepan of barely simmering water). Stir until chocolate is smooth and melted, and candy thermometer registers 110°. Pour 2/3 cup of the melted white chocolate into the foil covered pan and using a spatula, spread it evenly in the pan. Sprinkle with 1/4 cup crushed peppermints. Chill about 15 minutes. Meanwhile, stir the semisweet chocolate, cream and peppermint extract in a saucepan over medium heat until just melted and smooth. Cool to lukewarm, then pour mixture over the white chocolate layer (in the pan). Using a spatula, spread the semisweet chocolate in an even layer. Refrigerate until very cold and firm. Re-warm the remaining white chocolate in the bowl until it is melted again. Working quickly, pour the white chocolate over the dark chocolate layer; spread to cover. Sprinkle with remaining crushed peppermints. Chill and then cut into 2" squares. Store in an airtight container.

Put the candy squares into a jar that has been lined with a holiday tissue paper. Tie a candy cane onto the jar with a festive ribbon. For families with young children, include a copy of, "The Legend of the Candy Cane."

OLD FASHIONED BUTTERY CASHEW BRITTLE

Ingredients:

1/2 cup (1 stick) salted butter
1 cup of sugar
1 Tbsp light corn syrup
1 1/2 cups cashews

Directions:

Line a baking sheet with aluminum foil and spray with non-stick cooking spray, set aside. In a heavy, medium-sized sauce-pan, combine the butter, sugar, and corn syrup. Cook, stirring constantly over medium-low heat until sugar dissolves. Add the nuts and continue heating until the temperature reaches 290° on a candy thermometer (approximately 25 minutes). Spread the mixture onto the prepared baking sheet. Cool for 20 minutes. Break into individual serving size chunks, and store in an airtight container

For fans of brittles, this is one of the best! For a feminine look, place a doily into the bottom of a 1 quart glass jar and then fill the jar with brittle. Put another doily on top of the lid before screwing on the ring. Attach a pretty ribbon with a note and the recipe.

ROSE WEDDING MINTS

Ingredients:
2 1/2 cups powdered sugar
3 oz cream cheese
1/2 tsp rose water flavoring
1/4 tsp almond extract
Red food coloring

Directions:
Add all ingredients to a mixing bowl. Knead like pie dough until everything is thoroughly combined. Using a teaspoon, to keep sizes even, make small balls of dough and dip in granulated sugar. Press into a rose shaped candy mold, sugar side down, and unmold at once. Set on wax paper and then into an airtight container. Can be frozen.

These make an extra-special gift when given in a pretty little jar, tied with a with a ribbon, and bouquet of flowers. Look for candy mint molds at your local craft store.

EASY, NUTTY WHITE FUDGE

Ingredients:
2 Tbsp butter
2 lbs almond bark
1 8-oz package cream cheese
Pecans or walnuts, chopped

Directions:
Spray a 9"x13" baking pan with non-stick cooking spray. In the top of a double boiler, melt the butter. Add almond bark and heat, stirring, until melted and smooth. Meanwhile, as bark is melting, with an electric mixer, beat cream cheese until light and fluffy. When almond bark is smooth and melted, pour over the cream cheese and beat for 7-10 minutes. Fold in pecans or walnuts and pour into the prepared pan. Store fudge in refrigerator in an airtight container.

Place fudge in a glass jar. Set the jar in the middle of a piece of fabric, pull fabric up on all corners to the center top and tie with a ribbon. Tuck a card inside the fabric folds and include the recipe.

RASPBERRY POMEGRANATE FRUIT GELLIES

Ingredients:

2/3 cup carbonated raspberry soda, divided
2 1/4-oz packages unflavored gelatin
1 cup sugar
1 jar Raspberry Pomegranate Fruit Spread
Additional sugar for coating candy

Directions:

Line an 8"x8" baking pan with foil and spray the foil with non-stick cooking spray. Set aside. Pour 1/4 cup of the raspberry soda into a small bowl or measuring cup. Sprinkle with gelatin. Let sit for 5 minutes. Meanwhile, in a medium saucepan, combine the remaining soda with the sugar. Bring to a boil over medium-high heat and cook, stirring, until sugar dissolves. Add the fruit spread and whisk to combine. Return to a boil and cook until thick and syrupy, about 2 minutes. Add gelatin mixture and whisk until gelatin dissolves. Pour this mixture through a fine-mesh sieve into an 8" square baking dish. Refrigerate until completely set. When very firm, lift the gelatin out of the pan by lifting the edges of the foil. Place sugar in a pie plate or shallow bowl. Cut fruit jelly into 1" squares. Toss in sugar to coat just before serving.

Instead of regular sugar, toss these candies in a coarse, colorful, decorative, sugar "sanding". Then wrap each individually in clear cellophane before putting in a pretty glass jar.

CHOCOLATE MAPLE NUT BALLS

Ingredients:

1 8-oz package cream cheese
1/2 cup butter, softened
6 cups powdered sugar
1 tsp vanilla
1 tsp maple flavoring
1/2 cup pistachios, chopped fine
(reserve some for topping)
2 lbs chocolate bark, broken into chunks
1 cup pistachios, coarsely chopped

Directions:

Using an electric mixer, combine the cream cheese, butter, sugar, and flavorings. Add the pistachios, mixing in well. Chill, covered, for at least an hour. Remove from refrigerator and shape into 1" balls. Place the chocolate into a microwave-safe bowl and melt, stirring often. Dip the candy balls into the melted coating, then sprinkle with chopped pistachios. Set on wax paper to harden and then store in an airtight container.

Gently place the Nut Balls into a glass jar. Set the jar into a tissue or fabric lined basket, then pour a bag of pistachios in the shell into the basket to surround and cushion the jar.

HAZELNUT CARAMELS

Ingredients:

1 cup (2 sticks) butter
1 1/4 cups brown sugar
1 1/4 cups sugar
1 1/4 cups dark corn syrup
1 14-oz can sweetened condensed milk
1 vanilla bean
1 cup chopped toasted hazelnuts

Directions:

Line 9" square baking pan with heavy-duty aluminum foil, extending foil over sides of pan. Coat the foil with non-stick cooking spray. Melt butter in a large saucepan. Add both sugars, corn syrup and sweetened condensed milk, stir. Scrape seeds from vanilla bean into mixture; add bean. Increase heat to medium and bring mixture to a boil, stirring constantly, about 8 minutes. Using tongs, remove vanilla bean and discard. Continue cooking until candy thermometer registers 242°, stirring frequently, about 5 minutes longer. Remove from heat and stir in nuts. Pour caramel into the prepared pan. When cool, lift the caramel out of the pan with the foil. Using a buttered knife, score and cut into small rectangular pieces. Wrap each piece of caramel in cellophane and store in airtight containers.

DOUBLE-DIPPED CARAMEL APPLES

Ingredients:

4 Granny Smith apples (or your favorite variety)
4 popsicle sticks
1 14-oz bag caramels
2 Tbsp water
10 oz semisweet chocolate chips
2 Tbsp butter
A variety of toppings such as chopped candy bars, nuts, sprinkles, coconut

Directions:

Place aluminum foil on a baking sheet and spray with non-stick cooking spray. Insert popsicle sticks firmly into the apples. Unwrap the caramels and place in a microwave-safe bowl along with the water. Microwave in 1 minute intervals until it melts completely. The caramel should be a smooth, pourable consistency. Hold an apple by the skewer or stick and dip it in the liquid caramel, tilting the bowl and rotating the apple to cover it with an even coat. Repeat this with rest of the apples. Set all the dipped apples on the baking sheet. Place these caramel-covered apples in the refrigerator for 30 minutes. Meanwhile, mix the chocolate chips and the butter in a microwave-safe bowl and, stirring often, microwave until it is smooth and melted. Dip the chilled caramel-covered apples in this melted chocolate. While the chocolate is still wet, dip or roll the bottom half of the apples in the chopped candies, nuts, or sprinkles. Place them back on the baking sheet to cool completely.

Wrap each apple individually in clear cellophane with a ribbon at the stick. Put the wrapped apples into a large glass cookie jar tied up with ribbon.

MELT-IN-YOUR-MOUTH LEMON BALLS

Ingredients:

8 oz mascarpone cheese
6 oz quality white chocolate, about 1 cup of chips
(not white baking chips)
1/2 cup lemon curd
Shortbread cookie crumbs
Zest of one large lemon
1 lb white candy coating
A few drops of yellow food coloring

Directions:

Cover a baking sheet with aluminum foil and set aside. Place the mascarpone cheese in the bowl of an electric mixer and beat on medium-high until smooth and creamy. In a microwave-safe bowl, melt the white chocolate, stirring until smooth. Add in the lemon curd, cookie crumbs, and zest. Chill in the refrigerator for 1 hour, covered, until firm enough to scoop. Shape the chilled mixture into small balls; set the balls on the foil-lined baking sheet and put it in the freezer until balls are firm but not frozen. Melt the candy coating in the microwave in 30-second intervals stirring until smooth. Add a drop or 2 of yellow food coloring and stir to blend. Dip each ball in the candy coating and place it on the baking sheet. Let the coating set, about 10 minutes. Store in an airtight container.

Put the Lemon Balls into a small glass jar with a tight lid lined with yellow tissue paper or yellow gingham fabric. Attach a ribbon and the recipe and add a dried lemon slice to the ribbon.

DATE NUT JUMBLES

Ingredients:
2/3 cup powdered sugar
2 cups pitted chopped dates
1 cup dried sweetened cranberries or seedless raisins
1 cup chopped walnuts

TO MAKE GIFT JAR:
Spoon powdered sugar into a 1 quart jar. Add layers of half the dates, all the cranberries, all the nuts and remaining dates. Secure the lid.

Attach this recipe to your gift:

TO MAKE DATE NUT JUMBLES:
You will need:
2 egg whites
1 teaspoon vanilla extract

Preheat oven to 350°. Empty jar into a large mixing bowl. Add egg whites and vanilla. Mix well until dry ingredients are moistened. Spoon heaping teaspoons 3" apart onto greased baking sheets. Flatten to 2" rounds. Bake 13 - 15 minutes or until lightly browned. Cool on pan until set. Remove to wire racks. Makes about 36.

CRANBERRY OATMEAL COOKIES

Ingredients:
1 cup flour
1/2 tsp baking soda
1/2 tsp ground cinnamon
1/2 cup packed brown sugar
1/4 cup sugar
1 1/2 cups quick cooking oats
3/4 cup dried sweetened cranberries or raisins

TO MAKE GIFT JAR:
In a 1 quart jar, layer flour, baking soda, cinnamon, brown sugar, sugar, oats and cranberries. Cover.

Attach this recipe to your gift:

TO MAKE CRANBERRY OATMEAL COOKIES:
You will need:
1/2 stick (1 stick) softened butter
1 egg
2 Tbsp milk
1 tsp vanilla extract

Preheat oven to 375°. Empty jar ingredients into a large bowl. Add 1/2 cup softened butter, 1 egg, 2 tablespoons milk and 1 tsp vanilla extract. Beat at low speed until blended. Drop by rounded spoonfuls onto ungreased baking sheets. Bake 8 - 10 minutes for chewy cookies and 12 - 13 minutes for crisp cookies. Remove from baking sheets after 1 minute. Makes about 36.

TOFFEE TREASURES

Ingredients:
1 3/4 cups flour
3/4 tsp baking soda
1/4 tsp salt
3/4 cup brown sugar
1 cup English toffee bits
1/2 cup mini semisweet chocolate morsels
1/2 cup chopped blanched almonds

TO MAKE GIFT JAR:
Combine flour, baking soda and salt in a small bowl. Spoon into a 1 quart jar. Press brown sugar over flour mixture in an even layer. Add layers of toffee bits, chocolate morsels and almonds. Secure lid.

Attach this recipe to your gift:

TO MAKE TOFFEE TREASURES:
You will need:
6 Tbsp softened butter
1 large egg
1 tsp almond or vanilla extract

Preheat oven to 350°. Blend butter, egg and extract in a large mixing bowl. Add jar mix; stir until dry ingredients are moistened (mixture will be crumbly). Form into 1" balls. Place 2 inches apart on greased baking sheets. Flatten slightly. Bake 10 minutes or until set. Cool slightly. Remove to wire racks. Makes about 36.

MOCHA BALLS

Ingredients:
2 cups finely crushed vanilla wafers
1 1/2 cups powdered sugar
1 cup finely chopped pecans
2 Tbsp unsweetened cocoa powder
2 tsp instant coffee granules

TO MAKE GIFT JAR:
Spoon half the wafer crumbs into a 1 quart jar. Press into an even layer. Spoon in all the powdered sugar, all the nuts, remaining crumbs, the cocoa and coffee. Secure lid.

Attach this recipe to your gift:

TO MAKE MOCHA BALLS:
You will need:
6 to 8 Tbsp brewed coffee, cooled
Powdered sugar for coating

Empty jar into a large mixing bowl. Add 6 Tbsp coffee. Mix well until dry ingredients are moistened. Add more coffee if needed. Form into 1" balls and coat with powdered sugar. Allow to dry and set in one layer. Coat again with powdered sugar. Store in an airtight container to preserve freshness. Makes about 48.

CHOCOLATE WALNUT BARS

Ingredients:
1 cup flour
1/2 cup sugar
1/2 cup brown sugar, packed
12 oz (2 cups) semisweet chocolate chips
1/2 cup chopped walnuts

TO MAKE GIFT JAR:
In a 1 quart jar, layer flour and sugar, brown sugar, 1 cup chocolate chips, walnuts, and remaining 1 cup chocolate chips. Cover.

Attach this recipe to your gift:

TO MAKE CHOCOLATE WALNUT BARS:
You will need:
1/2 cup (1 stick) softened butter
2 eggs
1 tsp vanilla extract

Preheat oven to 325°. Line a 9" square pan with foil, extending ends over sides of pan. Grease bottom and sides of foil. Empty jar ingredients into a large bowl. Add butter, eggs and vanilla extract. Beat at low speed until blended. Spread in prepared pan. Bake 25 - 30 minutes until lightly browned. Cool. Lift from pan with foil. Cut into bars of desired size.

POPPYSEED CAKE

Ingredients:
3 cups cake flour
1 1/2 tsp baking powder
1/4 cup poppy seeds
1 1/2 cups sugar

Directions:
In a mixing bowl stir together the flour and baking powder. Spoon flour mixture into a 1 quart wide-mouth jar. Pour poppy seeds in on top of flour and then spoon in the sugar. Secure the lid tightly.

Attach this recipe to your gift:

TO MAKE LEMON POPPYSEED CAKE:
You will need:
3/4 cup (1 1/2 sticks) butter
6 eggs
1/3 cup milk
1 tsp vanilla extract
1 tsp lemon extract (not lemon juice)
Zest of 1 lemon

Preheat oven to 350°. Spray a Bundt pan with non-stick cooking spray. In a large bowl cream the butter with an electric mixer. Add the eggs, one at a time, then the milk, extracts, and lemon zest. Add the jar contents, and continue to beat on medium for 3 - 4 minutes until mixture is smooth. Pour batter into prepared pan and bake for 45-55 minutes.

Glaze: Combine 1/2 cup sugar and 1/2 cup lemon juice in a small saucepan over medium heat, and bring to boil for 3 minutes. When cake is removed from oven, poke cake all over with a wooden skewer and brush glaze over cake.

Add strawberry or raspberry preserves between layers to make a simple cake special.

DARK CHOCOLATE AND MIXED BERRY MUFFINS

Ingredients:
2 cups all-purpose flour
2 tsp baking powder
1 1/2 cups granulated sugar
1/2 cup dark chocolate, roughly chopped, or dark chocolate chips

Directions:
In a bowl, sift together the flour and baking powder. In the jar, layer half the flour mixture, half the sugar, and then half the chocolate. Repeat.

Attach this recipe to your gift:

TO MAKE DARK CHOCOLATE AND MIXED BERRY MUFFINS:
You will need:
1/2 cup (1 stick) butter
1/2 cup milk or buttermilk
1 egg, lightly beaten
1 tsp vanilla
2 cups fresh, or thawed and drained frozen mixed berries
1/4 cup raw sugar (optional)

Preheat oven to 375°. Spray muffin tins with non-stick cooking spray, or use paper liners. Pour the jar of dry ingredients into a mixing bowl. Melt butter in a saucepan over low heat, remove from heat and stir in the milk. Using a whisk, stir in the egg and vanilla. Pour over the dry ingredients and whisk to combine. The batter will be lumpy at this stage and this is exactly how you want it to be. Use a large spoon to gently fold in the mixed berries. Spoon the mixture into the prepared muffin tins. Sprinkle the tops with raw sugar if desired. Bake for 20-25 minutes or until toothpick inserted into center comes out clean.

CINNAMON CRUNCH BREAD

Ingredients:
1 cup all-purpose flour
1 Tbsp baking powder
1/2 tsp salt
1/4 cup brown sugar
1 cup whole wheat hot cereal, uncooked

Directions:
In a bowl combine flour, baking powder, and salt. In the jar, layer the flour mixture, brown sugar, and whole wheat cereal.

Attach this recipe to your gift:

TO MAKE THE CINNAMON CRUNCH BREAD:
You will need:
1 egg, beaten
1/4 cup butter, melted
1 cup milk
Topping:
1/4 cup brown sugar
1/4 cup all-purpose flour
1 tsp cinnamon
1/4 cup (1/2 stick) butter, softened

Heat oven to 400°. Spray 8'' x 4'' loaf pan with non-stick cooking spray. In a bowl combine the egg, butter, and milk. Pour the ingredients from the jar into a larger bowl, and whisk together. Add the liquid ingredients to the flour mixture, and stir until combined. Pour batter into prepared loaf pan. Combine topping ingredients (except butter) and mix well. With two knives or a pastry blender, cut in the butter until mixture is crumbly. Sprinkle topping over bread. Bake for about 20 minutes or until golden brown.

RASPBERRIES AND CREAM CUPCAKES

Ingredients:

2 1/4 cups flour
2 tsp baking powder
1 cup sugar
1/2 tsp salt

Directions:

In mixing bowl, whisk together all ingredients. Spoon into 1 quart jar. Seal lid of jar tightly.

Attach this recipe to your gift:

TO MAKE RASPBERRIES AND CREAM CUPCAKES:

You will need:
1/4 cup milk
1/4 cup cream
1/2 cup (1 stick) butter, melted and cooled
2 eggs
1 tsp vanilla
1 1/4 cups fresh or frozen (thawed and drained) raspberries, divided

Vanilla Buttercream:
1 cup (2 sticks) butter
2 1/2-3 cups powdered sugar
1-3 Tbsp milk or cream
Raspberries for garnish

Preheat oven to 350°. Put paper liners into muffin tins. In the bowl of an electric mixer, blend milk, cream, butter, eggs, and vanilla. Add jar ingredients and mix well. Mash 1/4 cup of raspberries with a fork and stir into the batter. Measure out and gently fold into the batter the additional 1 cup of raspberries. Spoon batter into muffin cups. Bake 20-25 minutes or until toothpick inserted into center comes out clean. Cool and frost. Put 1-3 raspberries on the center top of each cupcake as a garnish.

Buttercream Frosting: Using electric mixer, beat butter until fluffy. Add the powdered sugar and milk, 1 Tbsp at a time until proper consistency.

PEANUT BUTTER AND CHOCOLATE CUPCAKES

Ingredients:
2 1/4 cups flour
1 tsp baking powder
1/2 tsp baking soda
1 cup brown sugar
1 cup sugar

Baggie:
1 cup semisweet chocolate chips

Directions:
Whisk together the flour, baking powder, and baking soda. Spoon into a 1 quart jar, pressing down firmly. Layer the brown sugar into the jar and press down firmly, then add the sugar on top. Put the baggie of chocolate chips on top and seal the lid of the jar tightly.

Attach this recipe to your gift:

TO MAKE PEANUT BUTTER AND CHOCOLATE CUPCAKES:
You will need:
1 cup peanut butter
1/2 cup butter
1 cup milk
1 tsp vanilla
3 eggs

Frosting:
1/3 cup peanut butter
1 1/2 cups semisweet chocolate chips

Preheat oven to 350°. Line muffin tins with paper liners. Set aside baggie of chocolate chips from jar. In large bowl combine the jar ingredients with all the rest of the ingredients except chocolate chips and the frosting ingredients. Beat on low speed until combined; then beat 3 minutes at medium speed. By hand, stir in 1/2 cup chocolate chips. Spoon batter into prepared tins. Bake for 25-30 minutes or until lightly browned and toothpick inserted in center comes out clean. Cool completely, then frost.

Frosting: In small saucepan, melt chocolate chips with peanut butter. Spoon over cupcakes. Optional: sprinkle some chopped, salted peanuts over the frosting or put a chocolate candy on the top.

CLASSIC RED VELVET CAKE

Ingredients:

2 1/2 cups flour
1 tsp salt
1 tsp baking soda
2 cups sugar
1 1/2 Tbsp unsweetened cocoa

Directions:

Whisk the flour, salt, and baking soda together and spoon into a 1 quart jar. Press flour mixture down firmly. Whisk sugar and cocoa together and layer on top of flour in jar. Seal lid of jar tightly. Attach recipe directions (below).

Attach this recipe to your gift:
TO MAKE CLASSIC RED VELVET CAKE:

You will need:

2 eggs
1/2 cup canola oil
1 cup buttermilk
1 Tbsp white vinegar
1 1/4 tsp vanilla extract
2 oz red food coloring

Frosting:

1 cup milk
5 Tbsp flour
1 cup sugar
1 cup butter, softened
1 tsp vanilla

Preheat oven to 350°. Spray and flour two 9-inch cake pans. Set aside. In a large bowl, lightly beat the eggs with a whisk and then add oil, buttermilk, vinegar, vanilla and food coloring until combined. Pour the dry ingredients from the jar into the mixing bowl. Blend on medium until combined, scraping the bottom of the bowl once or twice. Pour the batter evenly into prepared pans. Bake 25-30 minutes or until a toothpick inserted into center comes out clean. Let the cakes cool for 10 minutes in the pans before removing to a wire rack. Cool then frost with Classic Red Velvet Frosting or a cream cheese frosting of your choice.

Frosting: In a saucepan, whisk milk into flour. Bring to a boil, whisking constantly, until smooth and thick. Remove saucepan from heat and cool. Then put into fridge, covered. Meanwhile, using electric mixer, cream together the sugar, butter and vanilla until fluffy (not grainy). Add the cold milk mixture to the butter-sugar mixture and blend until smooth. Spread between layers and on top and sides of cooled Red Velvet Cake.

SOUR CREAM SPICE CAKE

Ingredients:
2 1/2 cups flour
2 tsp baking soda
1 tsp ground cloves
1 1/4 tsp cinnamon
1 tsp salt
2 cups sugar

Baggie 1:
1 cup chopped nuts
Baggie 2:
1 cup raisins

Directions:
Whisk flour, baking soda, spices, and salt. Spoon into 1 quart jar and press down firmly. Put sugar on top of flour mixture. Top with baggies of chopped nuts, and raisins. Seal lid of jar tightly.

Attach this recipe to your gift:

TO MAKE SOUR CREAM SPICE CAKE:
You will need:
4 eggs, well beaten
1 tsp vanilla
2 cups sour cream

Topping:
1 cup brown sugar
4 Tbsp melted butter
4 Tbsp flour

Preheat oven to 350°. Coat 2 round cake pans or a 9" x13" baking pan with non-stick spray. Combine eggs, vanilla, and raisins from baggie. Let stand, covered for 30 minutes. Meanwhile, with electric mixer, combine sour cream and dry ingredients from the jar. Add raisin and egg mixture, and blend well. Bake for 1 hour or until toothpick inserted in center comes out clean. Spread with topping and bake another 10 minutes.

Topping: Mix ingredients together and spread on cake top. Sprinkle nuts from baggie all over top. Bake for an additional 10 minutes.

PLUM BUTTER

Ingredients:
1 vanilla bean, halved lengthwise
4 lbs ripe plums, peeled and cut into 1/2" wedges
3 cups sugar
1/4 cup fresh lemon juice

Directions:
Scrape the seeds from the vanilla bean into a 5 - 6-quart saucepan. Add the vanilla pod and the remaining ingredients. Slowly bring to a rolling boil over moderate heat (this will take about 15 minutes), stirring frequently. Boil, uncovered, stirring frequently, until plums are tender, about 5 minutes. Discard pod. In a food processor, purée plums with liquid in batches. Transfer purée to the saucepan and simmer over low heat, stirring and scraping bottom of pan frequently, until very thick, about 1 1/2 - 2 hours. The mixture should be about as thick as jam. Spoon the plum butter into jars, and store in the refrigerator.

HOLIDAY JAM

Ingredients:
1 cup fresh cranberries
1 10-oz package frozen strawberries, thawed
2 cups sugar

Directions:
Put cranberries in food processor or blender and process until a thick paste. In a medium saucepan, put the strawberries, sugar, and mashed cranberries. Bring to a boil and cook until thickened. Pour into jars and seal tightly. Store in refrigerator or freezer.

If you are using a canning type jar, slip a square of holiday fabric on top of the lid, under the metal ring. Screw the ring on and trim the fabric to your liking. Place a ribbon around the lid, slip a small ornament onto the ribbon, or a note card with the recipe, and tie it up with a bow.